Transport in VICTORIAN TIMES

Margaret Stephen

based on an original text by
Katrina Siliprandi

WAYLAND

Victorian Times

Christmas in Victorian Times

Clothes in Victorian Times

Schools in Victorian Times

Streets in Victorian Times

Sundays in Victorian Times

Transport in Victorian Times

How we learn about the Victorians

Queen Victoria reigned from 1837 to 1901, a time when Britain went through enormous social and industrial changes. We can learn about Victorians in various ways. We can still see many of their buildings standing today, we can look at their documents, maps and artefacts – many of which can be found in museums. Photography, invented during Victoria's reign, gives us a good picture of life in Victorian Britain. In this book you will see what Victorian life was like through some of this historical evidence.

Editor: Carron Brown
Designer: Joyce Chester
Consultant: Norah Granger

Cover picture: A Victorian horse and carriage.

First published in 1998 by Wayland Publishers Ltd
61 Western Road, Hove, East Sussex BN3 1JD, England.

© Copyright 1998 Wayland Publishers Ltd

Find Wayland on the Internet at http://www.wayland.co.uk

British Library Cataloguing in Publication Data
Stephen, Margaret
Transport in Victorian Times. – (Victorian Times)
1. Transportation – Great Britain – History – 19th century
– Juvenile literature. 2. Great Britain – History –
19th century – Juvenile literature. I.Title
388'.0941

ISBN 0 7502 1879 7

Typeset by Joyce Chester
Printed and bound in Italy by G. Canale C.S.p.A., Turin

Text based on *Victorian Life: Transport* by Katrina Siliprandi published in 1993 by Wayland Publishers Ltd.

Picture acknowledgements
Aberdeen University Library (George Washington Wilson Collection. Ref A123) 21 (top); Batsford 4; The Boat Museum 6 (top); British Waterways 5 (bottom), 6 (bottom); E.T. Archive *cover*; Mary Evans 10 (top), 11, 12, 21 (bottom), 23, 25 (bottom – Fawcett Library); Glasgow Museums: Museum of Transport 17 (bottom), 24; Howarth-Loomes Collection 10 (bottom); Image Select (Ann Ronan) 26; Jarrold Publishing 22 (top); London Transport Museum 15, 16, 17 (top), 18, 19 (bottom); Billie Love Historical Collection 13 (bottom); Manchester Ship Canal 5 (top); Mansell Collection 9 (bottom), 13 (top), 20, 27 (bottom); Hugh McKnight Photography 7; National Railway Museum 8, 9 (top); The National Tramway Museum 19 (top); Quadrant Picture Library 27 (top); Royal Institute of Cornwall 22 (bottom); Science Museum Library 25 (top); Rural History Centre, University of Reading 14 (bottom).

Contents

Moving People and Goods

Today, we have many kinds of transport and people can travel long distances easily. At the start of Queen Victoria's reign, in 1837, most people could not travel far from home. There were no trains, motor buses or cars. People usually had to walk from one place to another.

▼ This farmer walks his pigs to the market.

Moving Goods

Farmers walked when they took their animals to market. Horses and carts were used to carry coal. Coal was needed to power machinery in factories.

In early Victorian times, it was difficult to move goods from one place to another, but some people were lucky. If they lived near a river or canal, people were able to use boats or barges. Many canals had been built before Victoria became queen.

Digging Canals

New canals were dug out in Victorian times by navvies. You can see some navvies with their spades in this picture.

Mills and factories used canal boats to move their coal, wool, grain, wood and iron. Many canals were built across Britain.

◄ Navvies in Victorian times.

Canal Locks

Where canals did not cross flat ground, boats had to be raised or lowered from one level of the canal to another. Locks were built, such as the one in the picture. A boat entered the lock and the gates were shut behind it. The water level was raised or lowered. The boat sailed out when the next gates were opened. Boats had to fit into the locks. They were called narrow boats.

A canal lock. ▲

Canal Boats

In early Victorian times, canal boats were pulled along by horses. The horses walked on the towpaths beside the canals. In this picture, the boat is a barge. Barges are wider than narrow boats.

▲ The Leeds and Liverpool canal boat called *Tiger*.

Sometimes boats had to go through tunnels. There was often no towpath in a tunnel. People, called leggers, lay on their backs on the side of the boat with their feet touching the tunnel wall. To push the boat along, they then walked their feet along the tunnel wall.

Life on a Narrow Boat

Two restored and decorated narrow boats. ▼

Families lived on narrow boats. The cabins were very small. Usually, the children did not go to school. They helped with the horses. From the 1870s, narrow boats were often painted in very bright colours.

Steam Canal Boats

▲ This canal boat is steam-powered.

In late Victorian times, some canal boats had steam engines. By that time, canals did not carry so many goods. People used the new railways to transport goods. There are still old iron nameplates and signposts on some canal bridges and near canal towpaths in places such as Birmingham.

Railway Travel

In 1825, the first proper railway opened between Stockton and Darlington. Trains were driven by steam power. During Queen Victoria's reign, many railways were built in Britain. It became easier to move goods and to travel.

◀ The railway carriage used by Queen Victoria. The queen liked to travel by train.

Queen Victoria's Carriage

Queen Victoria's first train journey was in 1842. There were not many rail tracks in Britain then but, by the end of Queen Victoria's reign, nearly every part of Britain had a railway. One long train journey was to her castle, Balmoral Castle, in the north of Scotland. She enjoyed many holidays there. Her railway carriage was special and very comfortable.

The Cost of Railways

Building a railway was so expensive that many people had to share the cost. At first, the railway companies sold shares to people and used the money to build the railways. When the companies did well they shared the profits. Later, the profits were very small so people no longer wanted to buy shares.

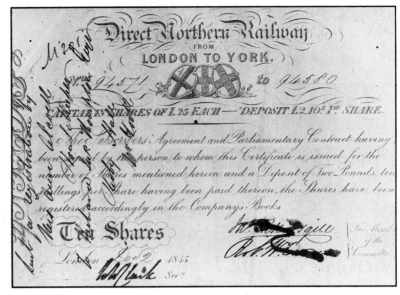

▲ Ten railway shares from 1845.

A railway accident near Beckenham. ▼

Railway Accidents

Many accidents happened when men were building the railways in Victorian times. Over 100 navvies were killed building the railway between London and Bristol.

There were also accidents when trains were running. In this picture a bridge has collapsed. In 1879, around 90 passengers were killed in a terrible disaster on the Tay Railway Bridge which blew down in a great storm.

Railways

Stations, such as Victoria station in London, often had high, glass roofs. Smoke from the steam trains made them very dirty places.

Trains brought food and other goods into towns. So more people were able to move into those towns to live. Rich and poor people travelled on trains. Some rich people went to work by train. People also travelled by train when they went on holiday. Poor people sometimes went by train for a day by the sea or a day in the countryside.

▲ This painting shows Victoria station, London, in about 1894.

A third-class carriage. ▼

Railway Carriages

Victorian trains had first-class, second-class and third-class carriages. Third-class was the cheapest way to travel. At first, third-class carriages did not have roofs. There was no heating on trains before the 1880s. The carriages were lit by oil or paraffin lamps. Later on, trains had gas lights.

Railway Servants

In the picture below you can see railway workers among the many travellers. They were called railway servants. Look at their uniforms. Sometimes, the railway servants lived in houses belonging to the railway companies.

This family at Waterloo station, London, have just returned from holiday. ▼

Horses and Traction Engines

In Victorian times, some people rode horses to travel around. Horses also pulled carriages carrying people, and wagons filled with goods. Later, machines driven by steam took over some of the work of horses. Now very few horses work for us in this way.

Stage Coaches

At the start of Queen Victoria's reign, there were stage coaches on the roads. They carried parcels, mail and rich people who could afford the fares. Passengers booked their seats at an inn. They ate and drank while they waited for the coach. On very long journeys the horses had to be changed at different places, called stages, along the way. When trains were invented, people no longer wanted to travel long distances by stage coach. Trains were faster, cheaper and more comfortable.

▲ A Victorian stage coach.

Carrier's Wagons

Carrier's wagons carried heavy loads of goods. They were much slower than stage coaches but cheaper. The wagons had wide wheels and were pulled by eight or more horses. The carriers walked or rode beside the horses. They carried long whips.

A carrier's wagon and horses. ▼

A family going to a funeral. ▼

Horses and Carriages

People often travelled on horseback in the country. Tired horses could be changed for fresh horses at inns. Rich people owned their own carriages and horses. Poor people had to hire carriages and horses for special occasions, such as weddings or funerals. In Glasgow, there was a station bus (a carriage) to take travellers from the railway station to their hotel.

Horses and Carts

Horses were used for work on farms. They were used to pull wagons loaded with crops.

Goods such as coal, milk and bread were delivered to people by horse and cart.

▲ Work on the farm, in about 1900.

◄ A traction engine at work.

Traction Engines

Traction engines were driven by steam. They took over some of the heavier work of horses. They could pull very heavy loads such as the tree trunk in the picture. They were only allowed to travel very slowly.

Horse-drawn Buses

From 1829, in London, Victorians could travel on buses pulled by horses. Only rich people could afford to use this kind of transport. A conductor collected the fares. Bus drivers worked a very long day. They started work at 7.45 a.m. and finished at about midnight.

A driver's duties were:
- not to let the horses gallop.
- to drive slowly, or at walking speed, in the markets and in the narrow streets.
- to drive the bus at least three feet (almost one metre) away from houses, where there were no footpaths.

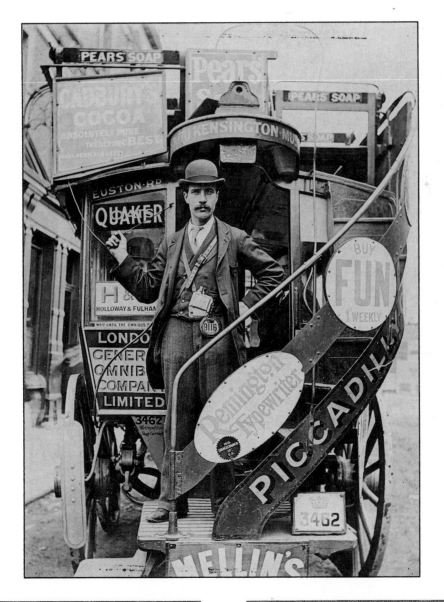

◀ The conductor on a horse-drawn bus in London.

City Railways and Trams

More and more passengers and goods came into towns. This meant that towns became very busy places. Roads became busier, with more traffic. Underground railways were built in London and Glasgow to take people quickly across the cities.

▲ Building an underground railway.

Building an Underground Railway

In 1863, London had the first underground railway in the world. Wide, deep trenches were dug out in the city. Then the track for the trains was laid down.

A roof was built to cover the railway. Houses were pulled down if they were in the way of the railway. Many roads had to be rebuilt.

Electric Tube Railways

Workers did not always dig trenches to build an underground railway. In late Victorian times, they were able to make tunnels deep down through soft earth to build tube railways. Instead of steam engines, electricity was used to power these tube trains. The coach in the picture had padded seats for comfort.

◀ A coach in a tube train.

Underground Cable Railway

In 1896, in Glasgow, the first underground cable railway in the world was opened. A tunnel was built under the city but the engines were not driven by steam and they were not driven by electricity. Instead, all the trains moved on cables pulled by one big engine that did not move. Trains gripped the cable to move and let go of the cable to stop.

▲ A poster for the Glasgow subway.

Trams

Tramcars were another new type of transport in Victorian times. Trams had wheels which ran on iron rails laid on the roads. Horses pulled the trams along smoothly. Two horses could pull 50 people on a tram. A horse bus, on a rough road, could only carry 25 passengers.

Conductors

Conductor sold tickets on the tramcars. The usual fare was less than 1p for 3 kilometres.

Almost everyone could afford to ride on a tram. If people wanted to travel on a tram they could stop it anywhere on the tram's route.

Steam Trams

Later on, trams had steam engines instead of horses to pull them. They went faster, but could not stop as quickly as a horse-drawn tram. Tram stops were used as brakes to help the trams stop and make journeys safer.

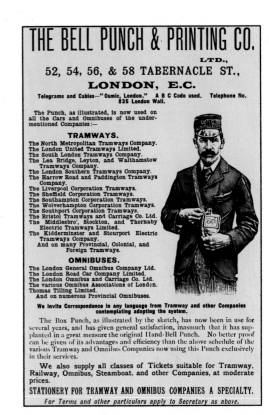

▲ An advertisement for a ticket machine.

▼ A model steam train.

Ships and Boats

In Victorian times, people and goods travelled in boats and ships up and down rivers and over seas. There were still many sailing ships during Queen Victoria's reign.

Sailing Ships

The Victorians built large, fast sailing ships. They were fast because their hulls were built of iron instead of wood. Sailing ships, called clippers, carried cargoes such as tea from China and wool from Australia. One of the best-known clippers, the *Cutty Sark*, can be seen at Greenwich, near London.

▼ A clipper called the *Cutty Sark*.

Cargo Carriers

In early Victorian times, paddle steamers carried some cargo. They could travel without the help of the wind, but they had less space for goods than clippers. Steamships with propellers were faster than paddle steamers. They carried more and more cargo. But, even at the end of Queen Victoria's reign, there were still many sailing ships.

▼ This photograph shows Aberdeen Harbour in 1882.

The *Great Eastern*

In 1858, a famous Victorian engineer, called Isambard Kingdom Brunel, designed a steamship, called the *Great Eastern*. It had a propeller, sails and paddle wheels. It carried 4,000 passengers and was the largest ship in the world at that time. If the engine broke down the sails could be used.

The *Great Eastern* steamship. ▲

Wherries

The boat in this picture is called a wherry. Wherries carried goods on the waters of Norfolk and Suffolk. The mast was near the front of the boat. When the boat came to a bridge the mast could be lowered. A wherry had one large, black sail.

Other parts of Britain had their own special types of boat.

▲ A wherry.

Ferries

▼ A ferry in the 1880s.

Bridges are built over rivers to allow people to cross. In Victorian times, ferries were sometimes used to take people to the other side of a river. People could row or pole the ferry across. On page 22 you can see carriages loaded on to a ferry. The ferry could also take horses.

▲ The Henley Regatta, in 1893.

Henley Regatta

Look at all these people in boats on the River Thames. Many are wearing straw hats, called boaters. Rich people watched boats racing at the Royal Regatta at Henley. Afterwards they rowed and poled boats themselves.

Bicycles and Cars

Rich Victorians had the chance to try new kinds of transport before poor people. Until the 1880s, poor people could not afford bicycles, and only the rich people in Victorian times could afford to buy motor cars.

Hobby Horses

Hobby horse bicycles were invented before Victorian times. They had no pedals. Riders had to use their feet to move the bicycles along the ground.

In 1839, Kirkpatrick Macmillan built the first bicycle with pedals. Afterwards, in 1868, people rode 'boneshakers'. These bicycles did not have rubber tyres and were very uncomfortable to ride.

▼ A copy of a Macmillan bicycle.

Penny Farthings

These bicycles were called ordinary or penny farthings. The wheels were like two coins. The penny was a big coin and the farthing was a small coin. These bicycles were lighter than earlier bicycles. They were difficult to ride. The long skirts that women wore made cycling harder for them.

Flora Thompson wrote, 'How fast those new bicycles travelled and how dangerous they looked! … it was thrilling to see a man hurtling through space on one high wheel, with another tiny wheel wobbling helplessly behind.'

▲ The ordinary bicycle, or penny farthing.

Rover Safety Bicycles

Rover safety bicycles were more like the bicycles we have today. They had a chain to the back wheel and were safer than penny farthings. Victorians could buy a safety bicycle for £10.

◀ This woman is riding a safety bicycle.

Riding Bicycles

By late Victorian times, many people could afford bicycles, either new or second-hand.

Some people paid for bicycle lessons. In some places, there were special tracks set out where people could practise. Men and women bought special clothes for cycling. New shops opened to sell bicycles.

People started to cycle to work. Shopkeepers used bicycles with large baskets on the front to deliver goods to their customers.

These people are learning to ride their bicycles. ▶

The Motor Car

Another new kind of transport in Victorian times was the motor car. At first, only rich people could afford cars. The one in the picture cost about £125 at that time. It looks more like a carriage than a car we would see today. The roads were rough and dusty. Men often wore goggles to keep the dust out of their eyes. Women wore veils to keep the dust from their faces.

▲ A motor car, from 1898.

◄ A Victorian street scene showing people making fun of the red flag.

The Red Flag

When cars were invented, people thought they were dangerous. So, until 1896, cars could be driven only if someone holding a red flag walked in front of them. This warned people about the cars.

Timeline

1830s

1837
Queen Victoria's reign begins.

1839
K. Macmillan builds the first bicycle with pedals.

1840s

1842
Queen Victoria first travels on a train.

1844
All railway carriages had to have roofs.

1850s

1858
Brunel's *Great Eastern* is completed.

1860s

1861
First street tramway service in London.

1863
First underground railway in London.

1870s

1870
J. Sturley designs the ordinary bicycle (the penny farthing).

1873
First sleeping cars on British railways between London and Edinburgh.

1879
First railway dining car service.

1880s

1884
Rover safety bicycle is invented.

1885
First successful petrol-driven motor car.

1885
First regular steam tram service.

1888
Dunlop invents the pneumatic (air-filled) bicycle tyre.

1888
Daimler builds the first successful four-wheeled motor car.

1890s

1890
Forth Rail Bridge is opened.

1890
First electric underground railway is opened in London.

1892
First British trains with toilets.

1896
Speed limit on the road is increased to 20 kph.

1896
Glasgow subway is opened.

1900s

1901
First electric trams in London.

1901
Death of Queen Victoria.

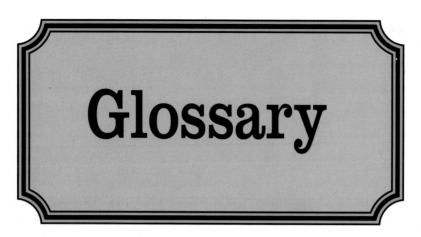

Glossary

Barges Boats used for moving goods.

Canal A waterway built by people.

Cargoes Goods carried by a ship or boat.

Carrier A person or thing that moves goods or people from one place to another.

Clippers Fast sailing ships.

Companies Groups of people who join together for business.

Hulls The main body of a ship.

Locks Parts of canals closed off by gates to control the level of water.

Navvies Workers who dug canals and, later, railways.

Profits When something is sold for more than it costs to buy, the extra money is called the profit.

Propellers Shafts with blades that turn to push a boat through the water.

Regatta A racing event for sailing or rowing boats.

Shares Pieces of paper, sold to people, that represent parts of a company.

Traction engines Steam-powered vehicles used to pull heavy loads along rough roads.

Veils Thin, see-through pieces of cloth that are worn over the face.

Books to Read

Macdonald, F., *A Nineteenth-Century Railway Station* (Simon & Schuster Young Books, 1990)

Tames, Richard, *History of Canals* (Wayland, 1996)

History of Road Transport (MacDonald Young Books, 1995)

Hicks, Peter, *The Victorians* (Wayland, 1995)

Places to Visit

Many museums have transport collections. Here are just a few:

England

Avon: Bristol Industrial Museum, Prince's Wharf, Prince Street, Bristol, BS1 4RN. Tel: 01272 251470

Birmingham: Museum of Science and Industry, Newhall Street, Birmingham, B3 1RZ. Tel: 0121 2361022
Birmingham Railway Museum, 670 Warwick Road, Tyseley, B11 2HL. Tel: 0121 7074696

County Durham: North of England Open Air Museum, Beamish, DH9 0RG. Tel. 01207 231811

Derbyshire: The National Tramway Museum, Crich, Matlock, DE4 5DP. Tel: 01773 852565

Devon: Exeter Maritime Museum, The Haven, Exeter, EX2 8DT. Tel: 01392 58075
Morwellham Quay Open Air Museum, Morwellham, near Tavistock, PL19 8JL. Tel: 01822 832766

Dorset: Bournemouth Transport and Rural Museum, Transport Depot, Mallard Road, Bournemouth. Tel: 01202 522661

Gloucestershire: National Waterways Museum, Llanthony Warehouse, The Docks, Gloucester, GL1 2EH. Tel: 01452 307009

Hampshire: National Motor Museum, John Montagu Building, Beaulieu, Brockenhurst, SO4 7ZN. Tel: 01590 612123

Lincolnshire: National Cycle Museum, Brayford Wharf, North Lincoln, LN1 1YW. Tel: 01522 545091

London: National Maritime Museum, Romney Road, Greenwich, SE10 9NF. Tel: 0181 8584422
Science Museum, Exhibition Road, South Kensington, SW7 2DD. Tel: 0171 9388000
Transport Museum, Covent Garden, London, WC2E 7BB. Tel: 0171 3796344

Merseyside: City of Liverpool Museums, William Brown Street, Liverpool, L3 8EN. Tel: 0151 3555017
Southport Railway Centre, Derby Road, PR9 0TY. Tel: 01704 530693.

Norfolk: Bressingham Steam Museum, Bressingham, Diss, IP22 2AB. Tel: 01379 88382
Maritime Museum for East Anglia, 25 Marine Parade, Great Yarmouth, NR20 2EN. Tel: 01493 842267
The Thursford Collection, Thursford Green, near Fakenham, NR21 0AS. Tel: 01328 878477

North Humberside: Hull Transport and Archaeology Museum, 36 High Street, Hull, HU1 1NQ. Tel. 01482 593902
Hull Maritime Museum, Pickering Park, Hessle Road, Hull.

Northamptonshire: The Canal Museum, Stoke Bruerne, near Towcester, NN12 7SE. Tel: 01604 862229

Nottingham: The Canal Museum, Canal Street, Nottingham. Tel: 01602 598835

Shropshire: Iron Bridge Gorge Museum, Blists Hill Site, Telford, TS8 7AW. Tel: 01952 433522

Suffolk: East Anglian Transport Museum, Chapel Road, Carlton Road, Carlton Corville, Lowestoft, NR33 8BL. Tel: 01502 518459

West Midlands: The Black Country Museum, Tipton Road, Dudley, DY1 4SQ. Tel: 0121 5579643

Yorkshire: Bradford Industrial Museum and Horses at Work, Moorside Road, Eccleshill, Bradford, BD2 3HP. Tel: 01274 631756.
National Railway Museum, Leeman Road, York, YO2 4XJ. Tel: 01904 621261
West Yorkshire Transport Museum, Ludlam Street Depot, Mill Lane, off Manchester Road, Bradford, BD5 0HG.

Scotland

Lothian: Linlithgow Union Canal Society Museum, Manse Road, Linlithgow, EH49 6HQ. Tel: 01506 842289

Strathclyde: Museum of Transport, Kelvin Hall, 1 Bunhouse Road, Glasgow, G3 8PZ. Tel: 0141 2219600

Wales

South Glamorgan: Welsh Industrial and Maritime Museum, Bute Street, Cardiff, CF1 6AN. Tel: 01222 485321

Index